LEADERSHIP

Off the Wall

Paul B. Thornton

WESTBOW
PRESS

WestBow Press books may be ordered through booksellers or by contacting:

WestBow Press
A Division of Thomas Nelson
1663 Liberty Drive
Bloomington, IN 47403
www.westbowpress.com
1-(866) 928-1240

Because of the dynamic nature of the Internet, any Web addresses or links contained in this book may have changed since publication and may no longer be valid. The views expressed in this work are solely those of the author and do not necessarily reflect the views of the publisher, and the publisher hereby disclaims any responsibility for them.

ISBN: 978-1-4497-0357-8 (sc)
ISBN: 978-1-4497-0358-5 (e)

Library of Congress Control Number: 2010931019

Printed in the United States of America

WestBow Press rev. date: 8/16/2010

This book is dedicated to
Owen Cohl Labor—A future leader
who no doubt will post great things
on his office wall!

Contents

Introduction

What are your guiding principles? What do you have posted on your office wall?

W. Clement Stone began as a shoeshine boy and became a multimillionaire. He credits his success to three words: **Do It Now.** He required everyone who worked for him to write those words on index cards and post them in their work area.

Over the past twenty years I have collected and analyzed many of the quotes leaders post on their office walls or keep on their desks. Many of these quotes, pictures, and mementos relate to a guiding principle they have followed to achieve success. In addition, I have also asked many leaders this question—"What is the best leadership advice you ever received?" This book includes a great collection of office wall quotes and advice about leadership.

This book will help you focus and further define your core beliefs, values, and guiding principles.

Chapter 1

The Leader's Attitude

Leaders have a positive, can-do attitude. They are optimistic and believe there is hidden talent in each person. Their enthusiasm creates energy and excitement. Leaders may get down from time to time but they never play the victim role. They take responsibility. They are confident in themselves and the people around them. They keep hope alive during difficult times. Presidential author and historian, Doris Kearns Goodwin said that no factor was more important to Franklin Delano Roosevelt's success than his confidence in himself and his unshakable belief in the American people. He had a remarkable capacity to transmit his cheerful strength to others, to make them believe that if they pulled together, everything would turn out all right.

"It can be done!"—Sign President Ronald Reagan kept on his desk in the Oval Office.

Dubbed "The Great Communicator." Reagan was known for his optimism and ability to express ideas in a clear, eloquent, and quotable fashion. He honed these skills as a radio host, actor, television host, and politician. In response to being dubbed the Great Communicator, he said in his Farewell Address: "I never thought it was my style or the words I used that made a difference: It was the content. I wasn't a great communicator, but I communicated great things...."

1

"Attitude is everything!" —Sign in red letters on the desk of Carol Leary, Ph.D., President, Bay Path College.

Carol states, "If we greet every day, every person, every goal, and every challenge with a positive attitude, I believe we can live a rich, full life and accomplish some extraordinary things."

"No Whining"—Sign on the desk of James Parker, former CEO, Southwest Airlines.

Leaders don't whine and complain. They don't play the victim role. Rather they face reality and deal with what is in front of them.

Bill Gates had a picture of Henry Ford in his office. It was there as a reminder to not do what Ford did. Ford said, "Any customer can have a car painted any color he wants so long as it is black." Henry Ford knew his customers wanted the option to buy cars painted grey, blue and brown. But he didn't think he had to respond to customer wants because he had a lock on the marketplace. This "fatal attitude" caused him to lose market share to upstart General Motors.

"Make It a WOW Experience!"—Sign in the office of Kate T. Labor, Vice President-Marketing and Customer Support, Systems, and Software.

Kate states, "Successful businesses exceed customer expectations. They get customers to say 'Wow' in response to their great products and services. Great leaders know if often takes a 'Wow' experience to get people excited and energized to pursue a new vision."

"Accentuate the Positive"—Sign in the office of the Ed Corcoran, Director, Integrated Disability Programs, Raytheon Corporation. He also has a wooden gavel on his desk. The gavel is inscribed—"Attitude Adjuster."

Ed states, "Leaders see opportunity in every situation. Negative people see doom and gloom. Leaders create energy when they affirm people's talents and focus on what's possible in the future."

"I'm Responsible"—Sign on the desk of Rudy Giuliani who was mayor of New York City from 1994-2001. During that time he was credited with major reductions in crime and improving the quality of life for all New Yorkers. He gained national attention for his leadership role after the September 11 attacks on the World Trade Center.

Leaders don't pass the buck, point the finger, or blame others. They take responsibility.

"It's not enough to say we are doing our best. We must succeed in doing what is necessary."—Framed inscription on the desk of Winston Churchill during the Second World War.

Separate "what" from "how." What needs to be done is one thing. How to get it done is something else. Leaders find a way to get the job done! Winston Churchill reputedly also kept the following aphorism on the wall above his desk: "Never, ever, ever, ever, ever give up."

"At least I now know that if the boss is a jerk, I have only myself to blame."
Deborah (Donaldson) Chamberlain, owner and president, Donaldson Media & Marketing Services, LLC, created her own office wall quote. She says that she only needs to read the quote every once in awhile.

Now that's keeping ownership where it belongs!

"I cannot give you the formula for success, but I can give you the formula for failure, which is—'Try to please everybody.'" Herbert Bayard Swope —Sign on the office wall of Paul Jenney, entrepreneur and small business owner.

Paul states, "At the leadership level it reminds me that not everyone will be happy when I challenge the status quo. At the business level it reminds me to focus. If you attempt to be all things to all people, you will not do well. Tom Peters said it as well, 'Stick to your knitting.' Know what you're good at, and deliver it 100 percent of the time."

"He who would be greatest among you must be servant to all." from the Bible—Sign on the office wall of Jim Camp, CEO & founder of Camp Negotiating Systems.

Jim states, "Jesus said that to His disciples. Ohio State coach Woody Hayes said the same thing to me and other coaches and students on numerous occasions. Coach Hayes practiced what he preached. Truly great leaders start by serving others. The next thing leaders do is inspire people to reach their goals. As a husband, father, grandfather and negotiation coach I try to live this every day."

"He who has a why to live can bear with almost any how." Friedrich Nietzsche—Sign on the office wall of Chip Conley, Founder and CEO - Joie de Vivre Hospitality and Author of *PEAK: How Great Companies Get Their Mojo from Maslow.*

Chip states, "I love this quote because it speaks to the importance of meaning in our lives. One thing I learned from Viktor Frankl (a psychologist who was in a concentration camp during World War II) was Despair = Suffering— Meaning. Suffering is almost like a constant in life, especially in a recession when many of us feel like we're living in prison. Yet, the variable that we should concentrate on is Meaning as the more Meaning (or Wisdom or Learning) that we experience—even in a difficult time—the less Despair we tend to feel."

"What is the largest room in the world? Room for improvement."—hand-written note on the yearly calendar of Greg L. Thomas, president, weLEAD Inc/Leadership Excellence, Ltd.

Greg states, "Leaders don't accept the status quo. There is always room for improvement. I have spent a good part of my career focused on self-improvement and on the growth of others."

Red L—Professor George Giarchi of the University of Plymouth – who is now 78 years young and still working has a large red "L" plate hanging on his office wall behind his desk.

George says that it reminds him to keep learning. He has always said that he learns more from his students than they learn from him.

"Winning isn't everything, but wanting to win is." Vince Lombardi —Sign on the office wall of Alan Hinkle, Sales Manager, Lockheed Window Corp.

Alan states, "If you truly 'want to win,' you keep digging until you find a way. Leaders have a high dose of wanting to win! They have great passion for their cause and their goals."

"Business is a matter of Human Service." —Sign on the office wall of Milton S. Hershey who was the founder of Hershey Chocolate Company and the company town of Hershey, Pennsylvania. He was a philanthropist whose core values included charity, modesty, and service. After his wife, Kitty, died in 1915, Hershey gave all of his shares in the company to a school for orphan boys that he and his wife had started.

"A life is not important except in the impact it has on other lives." - **Jackie Robinson** —Sign on the office wall of Kate Gordon, Vice President, Corporate Communications for the ATP. The ATP is the governing body of the men's professional tennis circuits.

Kate states, "Everyone wants to be inspired, whether they realize it or not. Leaders are those people who make us want to do more and do better."

Norman Love, Founder and CEO, Norman Love Confections

Norman states, " The best leadership advice I received came from Mr. Horst Schulte, former CEO of the Ritz-Carlton Company. He told me long ago to go to work with a purpose, to go to work striving to be excellent every day. In fact, to go to work to be better than you were yesterday. This is our philosophy, my employees and I, and has been since day one."

"Our attitude more than our aptitude determines our altitude." Zig Ziglar —Sign on the office wall of Jim Clemmer, author, speaker, and president, The CLEMMER Group.

"You are at home. You have arrived." Thich Nhat Hanh—Sign on the office wall of Marshall Goldsmith, executive coach and Founding Director, A4SL—The Alliance for Strategic Leadership.

Marshall states, "This reminds me to be happy now and not look for happiness 'out there' but realize that it always comes from 'in here' - inside of me."

Summary–the Leader's Attitude

Attitude is the frame through which leaders view problems and opportunities. In general leaders are positive and optimistic. They believe in themselves and the people they work with.

You're read the guiding principles related to "attitude" that several leaders follow. Now it's your turn. Create your own unique guiding principle related to attitude? Post it on your office wall. Solicit feedback from your core team. Do your actions match your attitude? What area needs improving?

Chapter 2
Communicate Big Ideas

Leaders have strong beliefs about what's important (priorities), what's right and wrong (values), and what changes are needed to produce a better future (visions). They take a position. They are not wishy-washy. Leaders have opinions, ideas, and proposals to improve the current situation. Rudy Giuliani states, "There are many qualities that make a great leader. But having strong beliefs, being able to stick with them through popular and unpopular times, is the most important characteristics of a great leader."

Leaders are effective communicators. They make their big ideas stand out. They eliminate the things that are of little value to their message. Leaders make their message concise—as long as necessary, but as short as possible. They simplify the complex but don't oversimplify. They use clear and concrete examples, stories, and visuals to make their ideas come alive.

Of course the other half of communications is listening. Leaders are curious and interested in people's ideas and opinions. They ask questions that point people in a positive direction. "What are the opportunities?" "What results are you looking to achieve?" "How can we improve the process?" They listen with their eyes, ears, and heart to determine what people are thinking and feeling.

"Be brief. Be Brilliant. Be Gone." —Former sign on the office wall of Mark Goodman, CEO, Twist Image.

Mark states, "While it's no longer on my office wall, it is something I try to explain to our team members at Twist Image. The ability for an individual to communicate in a clear and concise way is what will make them remarkable and even more credible."

"Start Talking and Get to Work"—Sign in the office of Alden Davis, former Business Effectiveness Consultant, Pratt & Whitney Division of United Technologies Corporation.

Journalist Alan Webber said that in the old days if the boss caught you talking on the phone or hanging around the water cooler, he or she would have said, "Stop talking and get to work!" However, in today's dynamic, fast-paced information society, if you're not talking with customers, colleagues, or suppliers, the boss is likely to say, "Start talking and get to work." Networking, blogging, listening, sharing, questioning, and discussing are the actions needed to stay current and continuously improve.

"A designer knows he has achieved perfection not when there is nothing left to add, but when there is nothing left to take away." Antoine de Saint-Exupery"—Sign above the desk of Michael S. Hyatt, CEO, Thomas Nelson Publishers.

Michael states, "Leaders remove the clutter so their big ideas stand out."

Ed Zimmer, Founder and President, Zimmer Foundation (TENonline. org)
Ed states, "The best leadership advice I received was--build your vocabulary. A large vocabulary allows leaders the opportunity to select the best words to describe the future, sell an idea, and influence people to change."

"Who else needs to know?" —Inscription on a paperweight on the desk of Karen Katen, President of Pfizer Global Pharmaceuticals and corporate executive vice president. She believes knowledge is a company asset, not the property of any individual. Katen applied the principle of knowledge dissemination relentlessly, thus propelling Pfizer to become a marketing powerhouse.

Leaders have an attitude of "openness." They believe information should be shared and utilized by everyone.

"Speak your mind—even if your voice shakes." Maggie Kuhn founder of Gray Panthers. —Author and thought leader Leslie C. Aguilar posts this quote on the wall of conference rooms when she conducts seminars and workshops on communicating respectfully in a diverse world.

Leslie states, "Leaders find the courage to speak up even when they're nervous. They know that one voice can make a difference."

"Use the "I" pronoun!" —Sign on the office wall of Sandra Levitin, Founder/CEO/Editor of kalonwomen.com.

Sandra states, "It reminds me to take a position. Take ownership. You can't be an effective leader if you don't have a point of view you're willing to assert and fight for. Women need to promote themselves and their ideas."

"Less Data—More Meanings"—Sign in the office of Thomas A. Goodrow, former Vice President, Economic and Business Development, Springfield Technical Community College.

Tom states, "Today we are flooded with studies, reports, and computer runs that provide data about every conceivable aspect of business. The amount of data is overwhelming. What's often lacking is a clear, simple explanation of what the data means. Effective leaders simplify the complex and make the meaning clear."

Hatim Tyabji, former chairman and CEO of VeriFone, Inc.
On his office wall there was a poster that consisted of twelve blocks, each with a photo of an Irish Setter. The first 11 blocks show the dog standing, oblivious to a command to "sit." Finally, in block twelve, the Irish Setter sits. "Good dog," reads the poster.

Hatim states, "That is the essence of leadership. I can't get disillusioned when I say 'sit' and nobody sits. So I just keep repeating the message. Leaders must be clear, consistent, and repetitive. Keep repeating the message until it sticks."

Michael Dell, founder and chairman of the board of Dell Computer, has a yellow toy bulldozer sitting on his desk. It is there to remind him not to roll over ideas that come from his staff.

Leaders are open to new ideas. They create a culture where people aren't afraid to state their views, ask difficult questions, and disagree with the boss.

Be curious. Dr. Mitchell Rabkin, former CEO, Beth Israel Hospital in Boston, had a small figurine of a little boy on his desk. The child is squatting, picking up something and looking it over.

Dr. Rabkin says that the statue was there to remind people of how important it is for everyone to be curious without any preconceptions. Asking questions, listening and learning are important activities for every manager and leader.

"Leaders are known for the questions they ask, not the answers they give." —Sign on the office wall of Steve Arneson, Ph.D. when he worked at Capital One. Steve is currently President, Arneson Leadership Consulting, LLC.

Steve states, "It was there to remind me to ask great questions, and lots of them. Leaders get caught up in telling, directing and making decisions, and generally don't ask for enough feedback or ask the really provocative questions that open up new possibilities. I didn't want to be that kind of leader!"

Brian P. Lees, Former Massachusetts State Senator and Senate Minority Leader
Brian states, "The most valuable leadership advice I've received came from my mentor, United States Senator Edward W. Brooke III. He told me to listen to all different kinds of people. Listening only to those who share your background and opinions can be imprudent. It is important to respect your neighbors' rights to their own views. Listening to and talking with a variety of people, from professors to police officers, from senior citizens to schoolchildren, is essential not only to be a good legislator, but to be a valuable member of a community."

"What You Notice Matters!" —Quote on the office wall of Melissa Wadsworth, Founder and President, Wadsworth Communications.

Melissa states, "I try to be aware and fully alert during every interaction with people." Leaders are present, in the moment. They focus on the here and now. Being present says to the other person—you're important!

"Put yourself in the other person's shoes." —Sign in the office of Doug Sills, CEO, Northern Louisiana Medical Center, Ruston, LA

Many leaders do what's called—Managing by Wandering Around. They spend time each day by directly talking with and observing people doing the work. They have a good sense of what others are thinking and feeling.

Debbe Kennedy is the founder, president and CEO of Global Dialogue Center and Leadership Solutions Companies. Above her desk are seven original paintings of Mother Teresa, Viktor Frankl, Martin Luther King Jr., Nelson Mandela, Mahatma Gandhi, Jalaluddin Rumi, and Eleanor Roosevelt.

Debbie states, "Each face watches over me as I work every day, creating an ever-present reminder of the importance of this journey of continuous renewal that we are all on at this time in history. I've always believed that we can remain in a continual dialogue with leaders like these shining examples if we are open to listen and learn from the wisdom they left for us."

Summary–Communicate Big Ideas

Leaders communicate their message in a clear, concise, and compelling manner. They are excited about their ideas, so they deliver the message with passion and conviction. Kevin Nolan, President & Chief Executive Officer, Affinity Health Systems, Inc. states, "What the people of an organization want from their leader are answers to the following: Where are we going? How are we going to get there? What is my role? The more clarity that can be added to each of the three questions, the better the result."

Leaders are also good listeners. They start by asking questions that focus on strengths, possibilities and a successful future. Their questions force people to look at things through a positive lens. Leaders make people feel that their ideas have been fully considered.

You've read the guiding principles related to "communications" that other leaders follow. Now it's your turn. Create your own unique guiding principle related to both sending messages and listening. Post them on your office wall. Solicit feedback from your family, friends and business associates. Do your actions match your guiding principle? Be open to feedback on how you can improve.

Chapter 3

Change the Status Quo

Leaders want to change the status quo. Change forces people out of their comfort zone. Leaders make their case for change by connecting with people at three levels —the head, the heart, and the hands.

- **The Head** – Leaders persuade people by presenting the facts and logical arguments. They present the hard data that supports their position.

- **The Heart** – Leaders persuade people by appealing to their feelings. What's in their hearts? They discuss the emotional aspects of their ideas and proposals.

- **The Hands** – Leaders persuade people through direct involvement – physical action. They engage people by having them try or experience a new approach.

Effective leaders create a sense of urgency and convince others of the merits of going in a new direction.

"I will change one life today!" —In the article, "Understanding the Importance of Rituals," author Justin W. Carter said that this sign was in the front office of a small company. As employees entered the office, they tapped the sign with their hand before walking in. This ritual instantly reminded employees of the importance of their mission and task.

Danny O. Snow, Author/Publisher and Journalist

Dan states, "The best leadership advice I received is a paraphrase of the famous 12-step prayer: 'God grant me the strength to change the things I can, the serenity to accept the things I can't, and the wisdom to know the difference.' I'm not too much of a drinking man, but I feel that this advice applies to so many other areas in life that it deserves consideration."

"All meaningful change comes from within." —Sign on the office wall of Nido R. Qubein, President, High Point University.

Nido states, "Leaders spend time in self reflection. They do the internal research to figure out what changes are needed. It's the internal changes that build people's confidence and self-esteem."

"Best Is the Enemy of Better"—Sign on the office wall of a middle manager at Milliken Company.

If you think you have the *best* training program, the *best* technology, or the *best* anything—what happens? You get complacent. Leaders think better--how can I do it better next time? That creates continuous improvement.

"Just because it worked once, doesn't mean it will work again!"—Sign on the desk of Shaun Coffey, CEO, Industrial Research Ltd., New Zealand.

Shaun states, "Every situation is different, and this is particularly so when dealing with change. People are different, and people change. An intervention that has been spectacularly successful may not work in a new situation. It may not even work in the same company/organization again because the people will have changed as a result of the experience. Keep changing your tactics, staying aware of how people are responding. Attack from different angles. Look for signs that something isn't working, and try something else—don't get stuck in your ways."

"Chance Favors The Prepared Person."—Quote on the office wall of Bettina Seidman, Principal, SEIDBET ASSOCIATES and President of Career Counselors Consortium.

Bettina states, "As a career management coach, I frequently talk with my clients about this concept. I believe that we all have to be prepared for whatever doors open next." Leaders prepare people to change. They build people's confidence and skills so they are ready, willing, and able to make needed changes.

"To every end there is a beginning." (David Tolpen, Laura's father) —Sign on the office wall of Laura Patterson, author, co-founder, and president of VisionEdge Marketing, Inc.

Laura states, "My father believed that even when something came to an end, a person's life, a relationship, a hobby, a consulting project, it created "space" for something new—a new and potentially better relationship, a new and as rewarding or better hobby, a new view on life, a new and potentially better piece of business or a new way to do business. Change creates new opportunities-new possibilities."

"And the day came when the risk to remain tight in a bud was more painful than the risk it took to blossom." Anais Nin —Quote on the office wall of Maria Marsala who has been a Wall Street trader, author, entrepreneur, trainer, and is currently a small business strategist.

Maria states, "In my life I have had several defining moments. These were times when I was in pain and knew I had to change. I learned it takes reflection, learning from mistakes and making important decisions. I had to identify which parts of my past I wanted to bring into the future. If you want to continue to blossom it takes courage and a willingness to unfold to the next level."

"Just for today...smile more; help others, be generous, work hard." (anonymous) —Quote on the office wall of Stacey Glaesmann, Licensed Professional Counselor.

Stacey states, "I like the quote because it focuses on today and is not as overwhelming as a total life change." Change often happens little by little, one step at a time.

General George Armstrong Custer's picture is on the office wall of Kevin Sharer, Chairman of the Board, CEO & President, AMGEN.

Kevin states, " It's there to remind me to:

1. Recognize and deal with reality. No leader can afford to delude himself.
2. Be coachable. Don't take criticism personally. When valid, learn from it and change.

"Give someone a W.O.E., A Word of Encouragement"—Sign on the office wall of Derrick Hayes, author, speaker, and thought-leader.

Derrick states, "Change is hard work. People need encouragement."

"Bring Energy!" —Sign on the desk of Maxine Clark, Founder and Chief Executive Bear, Build-A-Bear Workshop.

Maxine states, "Keep your eyes open. As an entrepreneur a big part of my job is to bring energy and ideas to every discussion, phone call, and meeting I'm part of. Leaders get people excited about new ideas, new possibilities."

Margaret Wheatley, Author, Leadership Guru, and president emerita of the Berkana Institute

Meg states, "I was interviewing a woman who had spent 40 years creating a very successful community. I asked her how she did it and she replied, 'Little by little, one step at a time.' I consider this to be the wisest advice I ever received about how change happens. It has helped me start things without worrying about where they're going. I just know that we have to begin. I also know that we don't serve our cause if we spend too much time developing a comprehensive plan instead of getting started. Those plans are bound to change as we get into the work. We do have to have a strong focus, intention, and will. And good relationships. Then we begin, step by step, little by little.

What's interesting about this advice is that I didn't receive it until recently. What it did was illuminate what I had also discovered doing my work and living my life."

Summary–Change the Status Quo

Managers use current methods and procedures to grind the Hamburg and get the job done. On the other hand, leaders want to change the status quo. They see possibilities and opportunities to do it better. Leaders not only talk about change but also make it happen. They start by changing their own thinking and behavior. Next they provide the roadmap, training, and support to help others change.

You're read the guiding principles related to "change" that several leaders follow. Now it's your turn. Create your own unique guiding principle related to change. Post it on your bathroom mirror at home. Each time you look in the mirror ask yourself—Do my actions match my guiding principle?

"If your actions inspire others to dream more, learn more, do more and become more, you are a leader."

John Quincy Adams

Chapter 4

Goal Setting—the Steps of Change

L eaders set goals that require us to change. They start by establishing long term goals. They then work backwards and identify all the actions and short term goals needed to achieve the new vision. The short term goals become the stepping stones of change. Sue Lewis, former executive vice president and chief real estate, The Travelers states, "I look for ways to push people out of their comfort zone, but not in a way that will paralyze them. Like throwing a rock in a pond, I try to stretch people one ripple at a time."

Without a stated goal, not much happens. Goals provide us with focus and motivation to achieve key results.

Klaus Kleinfeld, CEO, Siemens
Klaus states, "The best leadership advice I ever got was from an old friend of the family and it goes like this: Whenever you take on a new position, before you jump in and get bogged down in the details, sit down, lean back, close your eyes, and think about what you really want to achieve and how you want things to look in a couple of years. And only then—once you have a clear vision in front of your inner eye—start executing so that things will move in that direction."

"Debate the route only after agreeing on a destination" graces the bookmarks, writings, website, and lips of consultant, author, and speaker Ann Latham of Uncommon Clarity, Inc.

Ann states, "Far too often, people debate alternatives without first deciding what they want to accomplish. They leap to solutions without identifying the problem they hope to solve or the cause they need to eliminate. They argue about features without examining needs and requirements. I always start with the simple question: What am I or we trying to accomplish?"

"Begin with the End in Mind." Stephen Covey —Sign on the home office wall of Chris Bartley, Men's Varsity Basketball Coach, Worcester Polytechnic Institute.

Chris states, "I try to set goals that are clear and compelling—goals that help us improve and achieve excellence in all aspects of our basketball program."

"Be Realistic, Demand the Impossible"—Sign in the office of T. J. Rodgers, founder and CEO of Cypress Semiconductor.

Remember the old advice that goals should be challenging but attainable. No one ever said, "Set impossible goals." Impossible targets force you to think in new ways. If you had to increase your productivity by 80% what would you do? Doing more of the same—won't get you there. You must change your strategy—redesign your process.

Strive for Excellence. Signed photographs of Frank Sinatra, Mohammad Ali, Albert Pujols, Ted Turner, and Donald Trump are on the office wall of Jim Stovall. Jim is president, Narrative Television Network and author of *The Ultimate Gift*.

Jim states, "These are people who I've worked with and respect. They remind me to always strive for excellence."

Reach for the stars. Michael Neidorff, Chairman & CEO, Centene Corp. he has a paperweight on his desk of a hand reaching for stars. He explains that if you are reaching for the stars, you will never come up with a handful of mud.

Leaders pursue big goals and big dreams.

Wally Bock, Business Writer, Coach, and Consultant

Wally states, "Besides the usual pictures and such, there are two specific 'signs' on my office wall. Each is on a 3 x 5 card. One is my current most important goal, followed by the question, 'Will what you're doing right now help us achieve this goal?'The other is a reminder for when I'm writing. It says: 'What's the boss's bottom line?'"

Vincent Maniaci, President, American International College

Vince states, "The best leadership advice I received came from Dr. Jay McGowan, President, Bellarmine University. He told me that you may think you have ten things to focus on, but you really only have one or maybe two, and three at the most. Leaders need to be clear on the "big ideas" they are pursuing."

Brigitte A. Kirk, Director - Financial Planning and Analysis, Horizon Blue Cross Blue Shield of New Jersey

Brigitte states, "The best leadership advice I got was that no matter how daunting the task, leaders need to translate the complex into no more than three major points or action items that all stakeholders will understand. The application of this concept has been most helpful to me in achieving both my business and personal goals."

"#1 Priority is Company Culture"—Sign on the wall next to the desk of Tony Hsieh CEO, Zappos.com.

Tony states, "The best advice I got was from Robert Greenberg, CEO of Skechers, who told me that the most important thing in life is quality of life. At Zappos, our #1 priority is company culture. Our belief is that if we get the culture right and can help improve the quality of life for employees, then most of the other stuff, like delivering great customer service or building a long term enduring brand, will happen naturally on its own. Happy employees lead to happy customers."

"Super—Service!"—Sign on the office wall of Marty Topor, President Central Oil.

Marty states, "My goal is to provide great service. I try to deliver on every promise and commitment. My goal is to serve the needs of each and every customer. Building and maintaining strong customer relations is critical. When I have a disgruntled customer I can't sleep until the problem is rectified."

"Surround yourself with only people who are going to lift you higher." **Oprah Winfrey** —This quote is inscribed on a pillow in the office of Nancy Juetten, owner and president, Nancy S. Juetten Marketing, Inc.

Leaders surround themselves with people who have high expectations. These people set the bar very high. They challenge us to set challenging goals and pursue excellence.

Grizzly Bear —was on the office wall of Sarah Palin, former Governor, Alaska and VP-candidate in 2008. The bear was caught by her father. Sarah had it skinned with the mouth in a permanent growl.

I'm not sure of the precise reasons why Sarah had this on her office wall. But it reminds me of the significant risk leaders take when they challenge the status quo and pursue major change.

Summary–Goal Setting–the Steps of Change

Leaders pursue excellence. They pursue big ideas and big goals. Leaders establish goals that force us out of our comfort zone and require us to do new things. Achieving short-term goals keeps us focused and gives us a motive to keep going. Every successful leader knows the importance of setting the right goals.

You're read the guiding principles related to "goal setting" that several leaders follow. Now it's your turn. Create your own unique guiding principle related to goal setting. Post it on your desk. Each day check to make sure your goals are in alignment with your guiding principle?

Chapter 5

Confront Problems—Make Decisions

Leaders face reality and take on the difficult problems. They aren't afraid to make the tough decisions. Donald Trump states, "Great success rarely comes easily. Even today I encounter problems every day, but I remain positive, disciplined, and focused. Approach every day that way, and it's likely you will succeed. Adversity is very often an opportunity in disguise."

Leaders are willing to make the tough decisions which include:
- Changing the strategic direction
- Restructuring the organization
- Putting major resources behind a new initiative
- Firing non-performers

Leaders are able and willing to make timely decisions because they know what they stand for and where they are going.

"You can't help what you don't know." —Sign on the office wall of Dave Balter, CEO, BzzAgent.

Dave states, "Read, study, observe, listen. Be a student of the market. Listen to employees, customers, and competitors. It's a fast changing world. The first thing leaders need to do is understand the current reality."

"This too shall pass. Now would be good." —Sign in the office of Kate Lynch Bolduc, Chief Executive Officer, Greater Hartford Arts Council.

Kate states, "Big problems and big opportunities come and go. Effective leaders take action. They don't wait for perfect data or the perfect moment. They attack the issue and make a difference."

"Ask Why Five Times / Never Believe The First Report" —sign in the office of Kevin Podmore, Fleet Logistics Manager / Frito Lay North America.

The stated problem is often not the real problem. Effective leaders ask lots of "why questions" to identify the real underlying problem. They also ask "what if" questions to explore what's possible.

"A desk is a dangerous place from which to view the world." John le Carré —Sign in the office of Louis V. Gerstner, Jr., former CEO of IBM.

Seeing the problem, touching the part, talking directly with employees and customers provides a reality you don't get sitting in your office.

"Quit making stuff up!" —Written on a yellow sticky on the desk of Gayle Lantz, Founder & President of WorkMatters, Inc.

Gayle states, "At times I doubt myself or jump to conclusions about what I think a client is thinking, wanting or doing. In the absence of information, I don't really know. Leaders face reality—that means—get the facts, ask questions, and test assumptions. Find out what's really going on then take steps to improve the situation."

"Not everything that counts can be counted, and not everything that can be counted counts." —Index card tacked to Albert Einstein's office wall.

Some leaders only use hard data to define problems or identify new opportunities. Hard data—refers to the numbers. The numbers tell you what's happening with sales, expenses, profit, turnover grievances, customer satisfaction, and employee satisfaction? But the numbers often don't tell the whole story. Soft data is also important. Soft data refers to the hard to measure things such as employees' hopes, dreams, fears, and frustrations.

"Business as Un-usual" —Sign in the office of Cordia Harrington, President and CEO, Tennessee Bun Company.

Leaders aren't afraid to try something new. They experiment until they find a better way.

"Look to the greatness in others! Let go of the need to be right." —Handwritten note on a yellow post-it above the desk of John Hersey who is an author, speaker, and consultant.

John states, "I believe there is hidden talent and greatness in everyone. I try to uncover that greatness in every presentation, training session, and interaction I have. Another important aspect of leadership is being able to put my ego on hold and focus on what's right not who's right. These are the guiding principles my wife Beverly and I have followed for over 20 years as both business and marriage partners."

"The Buck Stops here!" —Sign on the desk of President Truman

Leaders take on the big problems and make the tough decisions.

"The most difficult thing is the decision to act, the rest is merely tenacity. The fears are paper tigers. You can do anything you decide to do. You can act to change and control your life; and the procedure, the process is its own reward." Amelia Earhart, aviator —Sign on the office wall of Marsha Friedman, Chief Executive Officer, EMSI

Marsha states, "As CEO of my company, I have a responsibility to lead and set an example for my team during both the highs and lows. Earhart's message of tenacity has helped me through difficult times. Believing that I can achieve whatever I set my mind to gives me the intellectual energy and determination to be able to persist."

Summary—Confront Problems—Make Decisions

Great leaders cut through the clutter and identify the real problem. They see problems as opportunities to improve the status quo. They aren't afraid to make decisions because they are clear on their values and beliefs.

You're read the guiding principles related to "confronting problems and making decisions" that other leaders follow. Now it's your turn. Create your own unique guiding principle related to confronting problem and making decisions. Post it on your office wall. Keep track—are you facing the difficult problems? Are you making the tough decisions?

Chapter 6

Take Action—Make it Happen

Leaders have a bias for action. They don't just talk about change, they make it happen. They start by changing themselves. As Indian philosopher Mahatma Gandhi said, "Be the change you want to see in the world." Leaders provide the resources and framework needed to make change happen. They take action by assigning tasks, setting goals, asking questions, monitoring progress, and celebrating success.

"Take Risks!" —Sign in the office of Carol Palady, PMP—Project Manager, General Dynamics Armament & Technical Products.

Carol states, "Do your homework, obtain details from your team, ponder the outcome, but by all means take risks. If you are not taking risks, whether the jumping off point fails or not, you are not moving the company forward. A good leader takes risks and learns from both the successes and failures of these attempts to succeed."

"I am only one, but still I am one. I cannot do everything, but still I can do something: and because I cannot do everything, I will not refuse to do something that I can do." Edward Everett Hale—Sign on the office wall of Michael S. Hyatt, CEO, Thomas Nelson Publishers.

Michael states, "I like this quote because it reminds me to do something. Leaders focus on what they can do, not what they can't do."

Remarkable Leaders make a difference! —Sign above the desk of Kevin Eikenberry, Chief Potential Officer, The Kevin Eikenberry Group.

Kevin states, "Every day I ask myself—*What am I doing today to help others be more effective and more successful?* Remarkable leaders add value to the growth and development of others."

"Whatever you can do or dream you can, begin it. Boldness has genius, power and magic in it." Goethe —Sign on the desk of Paula Russell, President, Time of Your Life Tours, LLC.

Paula states, "This quote reminds me to get started—take action. I also have a small round crystal vase with the words 'We can do this!' engraved on it. The vase was a gift from my partner. I try to always keep a few fresh flowers in this vase to honor the spirit of confidence. The quote and vase inspire me to persevere, and also to remember my dreams and my goals."

"Yesterday ended last night."—Sign on the office wall of John C. Maxwell, author and speaker.

John states, "It's not that you shouldn't rejoice over a job done well but there is always more to do. Leaders don't rest on their accomplishments. They keep moving the ball forward. Being action- oriented is a key requirement of every leader."

"The greatest pleasure in life is doing those things you have not done." —Plaque on the office wall of Jim Estill, former CEO, SYNNEX Canada.

Jim states, "Not sure who said it but I got it in a fortune cookie 20 years ago. It reminds me to take risks and venture into uncharted territory. Leaders keep learning and accomplishing new goals."

"Prove Your Groove."—Sign on the office wall of Peter H. Reynolds CEO/Owner, FableVision Enterprises.

Peter states, "It means don't just say it—do it. Show us your passion in action. Leaders use the media, storytelling, and technology to foster the development of each person's potential."

"When was the last time you did something for the first time?" Sally Edwards —Sign on the office wall of Leslie C. Aguilar, thought leader and author.

Leslie has another sign in her office that was painted by her friend Leanne. It says simply, "You can start." Leslie states, "I love these quotes because they remind me to take that first step towards an unknown when my inner voice urges me to stay where it's comfortable."

Leaders are willing to step out of their comfort zone and be the first to try something new!

"Focus, Face-Time and Follow-Through" —Sign on the office wall of Denis Orme, founder and president, Leadership Success Institute.

Denis states, "Leading change requires focus. Identify exactly what needs to change and be able to explain why. Face-time—you must deal with people face to face. It takes direct interaction to build trust and credibility. Follow-through builds momentum. People like doing business with someone who keeps his word."

Envision, Enable, Empower & Energize —Sign on the office wall of Mick Yates, founder, LeaderValues.

Mick states, "There are three steps in the Leadership journey. First, know what to do—that takes awareness. Second, do it—that takes courage and skills. Third, become comfortable with doing it—be authentic and deal with paradox."

"Successful People are the Few Who Focus in and Follow Through" —Sign in the office of Stew Leonard, Jr., President, Stew Leonard's Dairy.

Focus and follow through are important ingredients of success. Nothing impresses followers like a leader who keeps his or her promises.

"Will beats skill." —Sign on the office wall of Michael Smith, Esq., Vice President, Asset Management, Firestone Financial Corp.

Mike states, "Don't get me wrong, skills are important. But more important—leaders have an intense determination that is unwavering. They find a way to reach the goal!"

Nikki's Turtle Effect—Success requires a soft inside, a hard shell and a willingness to stick your neck out. —Sign on the office wall of Nikki Stone, America's first Olympic gold medalist in the sport of aerial skiing.

Nikki states, "My mother taught me this philosophy. I've used it to win an Olympic gold medal and become a successful motivational speaker and author. I'm proud to say my book, *When Turtles Fly: Secrets of Successful People Who Know How to Stick Their Necks Out*—has inspired others to go for the gold!

I've learned to be an effective leader you need a soft inside. You need to be in touch with your feelings and passions. A hard shell means you can't let negative comments deter you. Leaders commit to their goals, and develop the ability to overcome any adversity. Finally, leaders take risks. They stick their neck out. I took small steps—gained confidence, and then took bigger and bigger steps. Bottom line—The Turtle Effect has helped me be a leader in every aspect of my life. Thanks mom!"

"The Buck Starts Here!"—Sign on the desk of Donald Trump.

Leaders see opportunity and take action. Non-leaders only see the status quo and sit still.

Joan Goldsmith, Founder, Cambridge College and Author, Consultant, and Coach

Joan States, "As a leader and as someone who hopes to enable others to find the leader within themselves, I found the best advice for myself in the writings of Eleanor Roosevelt, our great First Lady. She observed: 'One's philosophy is not best expressed in words; it is expressed in the choices one makes. In the long run, we shape our lives and we shape ourselves. The process never ends until we die. And the choices we make are ultimately our responsibility.'

I evaluate my success as a leader by cautioning myself to avoid falling in love with my own words and instead to rigorously evaluate the results I've produced from my actions. I find that, as Mrs. Roosevelt has indicated, I create myself anew each time when my behaviors mirror my values and I realize my intentions through my actions."

Summary–Take Action–Make it Happen

Leaders are excited about the changes they want to make. They can't wait to get going and start implementing the plan. They provide training to help people gain the knowledge and skills needed for change. In addition, they provide the incentives and encouragement to motivate people to take the first steps.

You're read the guiding principles related to taking action that several leaders follow. Now it's your turn. Create your own unique guiding principle related to taking action. Post it on your office wall.

"Leadership is lifting a person's vision
to higher sights, the raising of a person's
performance to a higher standard,
the building of a personality beyond
its normal limitations."

Peter F. Drucker

Chapter 7

Live Your Values

Leaders practice what they preach. They have alignment with what they think, say, and do. They are authentic and open about who they are and what they believe. Leaders have great credibility and that makes them influential.

"The time is always right to do what is right." Martin Luther King Jr. —Sign on the office wall of Michael Jansma, President GEMaffair.com.

Leaders consistently stand up for their values and beliefs. It's not a once in awhile thing.

Learning, Honesty, Integrity, Respect —Sign on the office wall of Kevin Drumm, PhD, President Broome Community College.

Kevin states, "These are values of the college. On a day to day basis I try to live these values by communicating from the heart, walking the talk, and not shooting the messenger."

Simple Trust —Sign of the office wall of Trevor Gay who is an author and consultant.

Trevor states, "I trust the people who follow me. I've always tried to demonstrate to anyone who has had me as a boss that I trust them to make the right call. In my experience, giving front line folks the trust they deserve works—we all feel better for it, and we all achieve things together."

"Leaders should be able to Stand Alone, Take the Heat, Bear the Pain, Tell the Truth, and Do What's Right" Max DePree —Sign in the office of Brian Morehouse, coach of women's basketball at Hope College, 2006 Division III National Champions.

Brian states, "That quote covers everything a leader needs to do as they approach their day in terms of courage, integrity, focus, and perseverance. And, it closely meshes with my coaching philosophy which is –Do the right thing every day, every play, on and off the court!"

"Integrity is never being ashamed of your reflection." —This quote is on the office wall of David Cottrell, founder and president of CornerStone Leadership Institute.

Every follower wants to know—is this leader credible? Does he say what he really thinks? Do his actions match his words?

Dr. Andrew M. Scibelli, President Emeritus, Springfield Technical Community College

Andy states, "The best leadership advice I received came from my father by word and deed. His words and actions consistently demonstrated the following: 'Always treat people with respect. Never compromise your integrity. And be open, honest, and candid at all times, but temper your candor with compassion and understanding.'

Simple and sound advice that has served me well."

"Don't do anything that wouldn't make your MOM proud." —Plaque on the office wall of Ursula M. Burns, CEO Xerox.

Early in life, we often accept the values and expectations of our parents, and other significant people in our lives. But, at some point leaders ask —what do I really value? What are my core beliefs? The clarity of the answers to these questions tends to evolve over time. In some cases—mom or dad had it right. Their values and expectations become our values and expectations. Bottom line—all great leaders know what they stand for.

"Practice, then Preach" —Sign in the office of Mary Jean Thornton, a former Executive Vice President, The Travelers.

Mary Jean states, "The most effective leaders set a clear and powerful example for others to follow."

Teamwork! —Sign on the office wall of Edgar Alejandro, Manager-Economic and Community Development, Western Massachusetts Electric Company. Edgar was also the hockey coach of two-time state champions, Cathedral High School.

Edgar states, "This sign reminds me to make connections--network. Working as a team we can accomplish great things. Let the spotlight shine on others. Help others achieve their goals."

"Faith" —Sign on the office wall of Daryl Wizelman, former CEO of United Pacific Mortgage and Mandalay Mortgage and currently an inspirational speaker.

Daryl states, "I am not religious but I do have a great deal of faith. This is a handwritten note given to me by my brother Randy during a very dark time in my life after my business was sold to Countrywide in 2007. It has been pinned to the bulletin board in my office ever since. It reminds me that life and business are full of up's and downs but in the end I must have faith in myself, the people around me and the world we live in."

Gerry FitzGerald, President, FitzGerald & Mastroianni Advertising, Inc.

Gerry states, "I've never put up signs on the wall or on my desk because I've always felt motivational messages work best when they're private.

"But I do have a sign. It's right up there on the front wall of my brain where I can't avoid it. I see it every morning and whenever I'm engaged in any sort of introspection. It's a simple message that I heard somewhere many years ago and said 'that's the one to keep with you for life.' It's all about personal integrity but when you embrace it fully, as I do, it applies to every facet of personal and business life.

It is 'Do the right thing when nobody's looking.' It's simple enough for even me to remember and call on every day."

"Love your neighbor as yourself" —Sign on the office wall of Sen. Sam Brownback (R-KS), a leading social and fiscal conservative.

Do leaders love their followers? In their book, *Leadership Challenge*, authors Jim Kouzes and Barry Posner found that many leaders used the word love when talking about their own motivation to lead.

Summary–Live Your Values

Pure and simple, but not always easy to do—leaders live their values. That makes them authentic and credible. Unfortunately some leaders don't walk the talk. Erik Lie, finance professor at the University of Iowa, has a framed single share of Enron Corp. stock on his office wall. The stock was purchased in 2002 when the stock value hit rock bottom. Below the stock there is an inscription of the company's proclaimed values—"Respect— Integrity—Communication—Excellence." Several Enron leaders didn't live the company values.

You're read the guiding principles related to living your values. Now it's your turn. Create your own unique guiding principle related to living your values. Post it on your computer. Each week take some time to reflect on how well you are living your values.

Chapter 8

Summary—Leadership Off the Wall

The signs in my office are "Be the Leader, Make the difference." It's actually the title of a book I previously wrote. It reminds me to have an opinion, speak up, and take a stand. The other quote in my office is "Childlike Qualities We Should All Keep—Curiosity, Playfulness, and Fun." It reminds me that leaders have a sense of humor. They take on serious tasks but have fun doing it.

What can you do to become a more effective leader?

1. Think about the type of leader you want to be. Write down your guiding principles.
2. Revise and update your principles as needed.
3. Take time to think about how well you are practicing your leadership principles.
4. Realize you have blind spots. Be open. Solicit feedback from bosses, peers, employees and significant others to identify your strengths and improvement opportunities.
5. Practice continuous improvement.

Becoming an effective leader is a life-long journey. There are always new things to learn and apply regarding:
- Having the attitude of a leader
- Communicating big ideas
- Changing the status quo

- Setting goals
- Confronting problems
- Making decisions
- Taking action
- Living your values

Be a Great Leader, Make a Big Difference!

About the Author

Paul B. Thornton is a speaker, author, consultant, and professor of business administration at Springfield Technical Community College. In addition, he is an associate professor at large for the Thierry Graduate School of Leadership located in Brussels, Belgium.

Paul is president, Be The Leader Associates. His company designs and conducts management/leadership programs for many companies, including Mercy Health Systems, Palmer Foundry, UMASS Medical School, Management Development International, Kuwait Oil Corporation, Young Presidents Organization, and United Technologies Corporation.

His most popular half day seminars include:
- Management and Leadership Styles
- Be the Leader, Make the Difference
- Implementing Change
- Dealing with Difficult People

He is the author of numerous articles and 13 books on management and leadership. His latest books include:

- *Leadership-Best Advice I Ever Got*
- *The Big Three Management Styles*
- *Big Leadership Ideas*

Contact information
www.PBThornton.com
PThornton@stcc.edu

www.ingramcontent.com/pod-product-compliance
Lightning Source LLC
Chambersburg PA
CBHW051252170526
45165CB00004B/1688